FOREST BATHING RETREAT

FOREST BATHING RETREAT

Find Wholeness *in the* Company *of* Trees

HANNAH FRIES

Storey Publishing

The mission of Storey Publishing is to serve our customers by publishing practical information that encourages personal independence in harmony with the environment.

EDITED BY Liz Bevilacqua
ART DIRECTION AND BOOK DESIGN BY Carolyn Eckert
TEXT PRODUCTION BY Erin Dawson

COVER PHOTOGRAPHY BY Andrew Walton/Unsplash, back flap; Anton Darius Sollers/Unsplash, **front**, t.l.; © Carl Johan Johansson, **front**, b.l.; Grant McCurdy/Unsplash, **front flap**; Ian Schneider/Unsplash, Author photo: © Susan Quinn; **inside back**; © Nate & Amanda Howard/Stocksy United, **back**; Kazuend/Unsplash, **inside front**; Remi Walle/Unsplash, **spine**, top; Rodion Kutsaev/Unsplash, **front**, t.r. and **spine**, b.; © Stephen Matera, **front**, b.r.

ADDITIONAL PHOTOGRAPHY CREDITS ON PAGE 191

ILLUSTRATIONS © Amy Stafford, Blixa 6 Studios, 9–12, 15–19, 66, 81, 85, 91, 93, 102, 122, 129, 143, 153, 165; © Elisabeth Fredriksson, 20–21, 56–57, 108–109, 144–145; Ilona Sherratt, 29, 41, 61, 70–71, 76, 97, 117, 132, 138–139, 150, 161, 163, 169, 177, 183, 185

Storey Publishing
210 MASS MoCA Way
North Adams, MA 01247
storey.com

Printed in China by Toppan Leefung Printing Ltd.
10 9 8 7 6 5 4 3 2 1

Library of Congress Cataloging-in-Publication Data

Names: Fries, Hannah, author.
Title: Forest bathing retreat : find wholeness in the company of trees /
Hannah Fries.
Description: North Adams, MA : Storey Publishing, 2018.
Identifiers: LCCN 2018012740 (print) | LCCN 2018017016 (ebook) | ISBN 9781635860955 (ebook) | ISBN 9781635860948 (paper with flaps : alk. paper)
Subjects: LCSH: Forest reserves—Therapeutic use. | Nature, Healing power of. | Mind and body.
Classification: LCC RZ999 (ebook) | LCC RZ999 .F75 2018 (print) | DDC
615.8/515—dc23
LC record available at https://lccn.loc.gov/2018012740

dedicated to my parents, dendrophiles both

It is not so much for its beauty
that the forest makes a claim
upon men's hearts, as for that
subtle something, that quality of air
that emanates from old trees,
that so wonderfully changes and
renews a weary spirit.

— Robert Louis Stevenson

BREATHE

21

CONNECT

57

HEAL
109
give
THANKS
144

Foreword

ROBIN WALL KIMMERER

Author of *Braiding Sweetgrass*

My daily calendar is filled with appointments and classes; and, if I were so inclined, I could calculate the number of lifetime hours I have spent in meetings . . . or on a conference call or answering email. I most emphatically do not want to know that number, which would only make me cringe and send me wailing out the door. The tally I really care about is how many cumulative months I have spent in the company of trees. I believe the number would total years, hopefully decades, that I have spent botanizing, birding, hiking, camping, picking berries, digging medicines, gathering firewood, teaching, doing science, or working toward some other purposeful woodland pursuit. Often during these outdoor activities I am interrupted by the imperative of more important tasks — like sitting on a stone wall watching clouds or a balsamiferous afternoon spent lying on my stomach in deep pine needles listening for centipede footfalls on a moss carpet. As it turns out, I have spent a lifetime engaging in "forest therapy," all the while thinking I was just playing in the woods. My mother, endlessly emptying my pockets of stones and seedpods, despairing of my muddy knees and elbows (which I still sport as a grandmother), would be relieved to know that what she called "daydreaming in the woods" is now called "forest bathing" — though I never came home clean!

What was once as natural as breathing, to be in the presence of trees and birds and that elegant walking stick insect masquerading as a twig, has vanished from many lives. Today, most of us live in cities and the hours in front of a screen vastly surpass the hours beneath leaves. How many miles do we walk without our feet ever touching the softness of the forest floor? What green spaces we do have are often manicured playgrounds, shaped to our will. We have constructed barriers around our lives, sealed in plastic wrap as if insulating ourselves from the living, breathing, gorgeously teeming world.

Forest Bathing Retreat is an invitation from Hannah Fries to become "more permeable to the natural world around you."

The name "forest bathing" arose from an understanding of the deep therapeutic benefits, both physical and spiritual, of being in the company of trees. It is a translation of the Japanese term *shinrin-yoku,* coined in the 1980s as a form of forest therapy to treat the many ailments which arise from urban life, calendars full of stress, and pavement beneath our feet.

I can attest to its soul-filling qualities. There is a vibrant reciprocity between the leaves and birds and seemingly silent trunks and the warm-blooded human sitting on the log, an exchange of mutual knowing that we are made lonely without. Like the health-giving benefits of bathing in mineral springs that spawned an era of "taking the waters" in resorts and clinics, forest bathing is a sensory immersion in green light and birdsong that leaves the bather renewed and clean.

I am blessed to have spent a life in the woods, but if the woods are out of reach, you can saunter through the pages here. This handsome volume invites you to be fully intentional, not to walk through the woods in order to get somewhere, but with the sole purpose of being fully present to yourself and to the lives around you. In sections labeled Breathe, Connect, Heal, and Give Thanks, Fries invites a deeper connection to the natural world.

Like the skilled and graceful editor she is, Fries has curated a collection of literary prose and poetry and evocative forest images that invite you to slow down and connect deeply with each sense fully tuned to the tone of the forest. She takes your hand and guides you down a winding path of wonder that offers peace and companionship of the forest world. Like the dendrophile she is, she has chosen words and images that play together like sunflecks through the treetops. Like the gifted poet she is, she bestows delicious words that we didn't know we needed, offering a prescription for our minimum daily requirement of *psithurism,* a rich draught of *petrichor,* and the soothing medicine of *komorebi.* You will feel lighter at the end of your walk with Hannah Fries.

IN THE COMPANY OF TREES

Rustling leaves.
Creaking trunks.
The green smell of the earth after a light rain.
Sunlight falling through the lacework of leaves.

Just reading a description of being in the forest might make you pause, take a deep breath, feel the soft edge of peace that comes from spending time outdoors. You remember the feeling. Perhaps it's been a while, or perhaps just yesterday you gave yourself a few minutes on a mossy rock. Either way, it tugs at you, asks you to return.

Being in the woods doesn't just *feel* good but is, in fact, good for you. If you've ever spent time in the forest yourself, you probably don't need a scientist to tell you that. Having grown up exploring the woods and climbing the trees of New Hampshire, the idea seems, well, natural to me. My first climbing trees, the crab apple in our front yard and the red maple in our backyard, were like old friends. Depending on my mood, they offered comfort, exhilaration, or peace.

Hand-in-hand with my love for the woods came my love for literature about the natural world. People have been going to nature for solace and healing for a very long time, and they have been putting words to that relationship for maybe just as long. And it's not only the woods they turn to, of course. Some go to the desert, some to the sea, some to a wide sweep of prairie.

Who's to say
why our spirits
feel at home
in a particular place?

This book, however, is for those of us who love the company of trees. You will find writings here from Native American traditions, Japanese haiku masters, the Romantics of nineteenth-century Europe, American Transcendentalists, voices of the modern environmental movement, and others. You will find the famous American walker, Henry David Thoreau, who "frequently tramped eight or ten miles through the deepest snow to keep an appointment with a beech-tree, or a yellow-birch, or an old acquaintance among the pines."

Like many schoolchildren, I read the work of Thoreau, Ralph Waldo Emerson, and Walt Whitman when I was about 15. Perhaps unlike most schoolchildren, however, I felt an intense connection with the American Transcendentalists we were learning about. I recognized the urge to run to the woods to escape society or for comfort when I felt low, and I remember feeling rather pleased with myself for hauling my reading as high as I could to a nook in the red maple so I could absorb it in the appropriate context.

Now, as a poet, I find inspiration not only in the beauty of nature but also in the fascinating revelations of science and the mysteries science has yet to (and, in some cases, may never) unravel. This book is a testament to all of this. It also takes as a jumping-off point the concept of "forest bathing," a term that may be new to us, but something I feel like I've been doing in one way or another all my life. It is simply the newest iteration of a long-felt truth with deep roots that extend to many traditions around the world.

The Japanese government coined the term "forest bathing" (*shinrin-yoku* in Japanese) in the 1980s to describe the practice of spending time in the woods to soak up its health benefits. It does not involve water (unless you feel inclined to dip yourself in a stream or pond, in which case, by all means!), and it does not require strenuous exercise (we don't all have to cover the miles that Thoreau did). Think, rather, of a slow, leisurely stroll, a pace that gives you time to notice small things, like a caterpillar crawling across a leaf or the unique scent of a pine forest — time to open your senses to the world around you. "Attention is the beginning of devotion," wrote beloved nature poet Mary Oliver — a practice out of which grows reverence, yes, but also healing and connection. And as Ralph Waldo Emerson wrote, "In the woods we return to reason and to faith." You will find in this book myriad variations on these sentiments, from ancient to modern, from religious to scientific.

Only relatively recently in evolutionary history have so many of us humans lived largely indoors — is it any wonder that our bodies, minds, and souls crave the outdoors? May the readings in this book draw you to the woods, remind you of the sensory experiences you encounter there, and encourage you to find your own wholeness and wildness among the trees.

— *Hannah Fries*

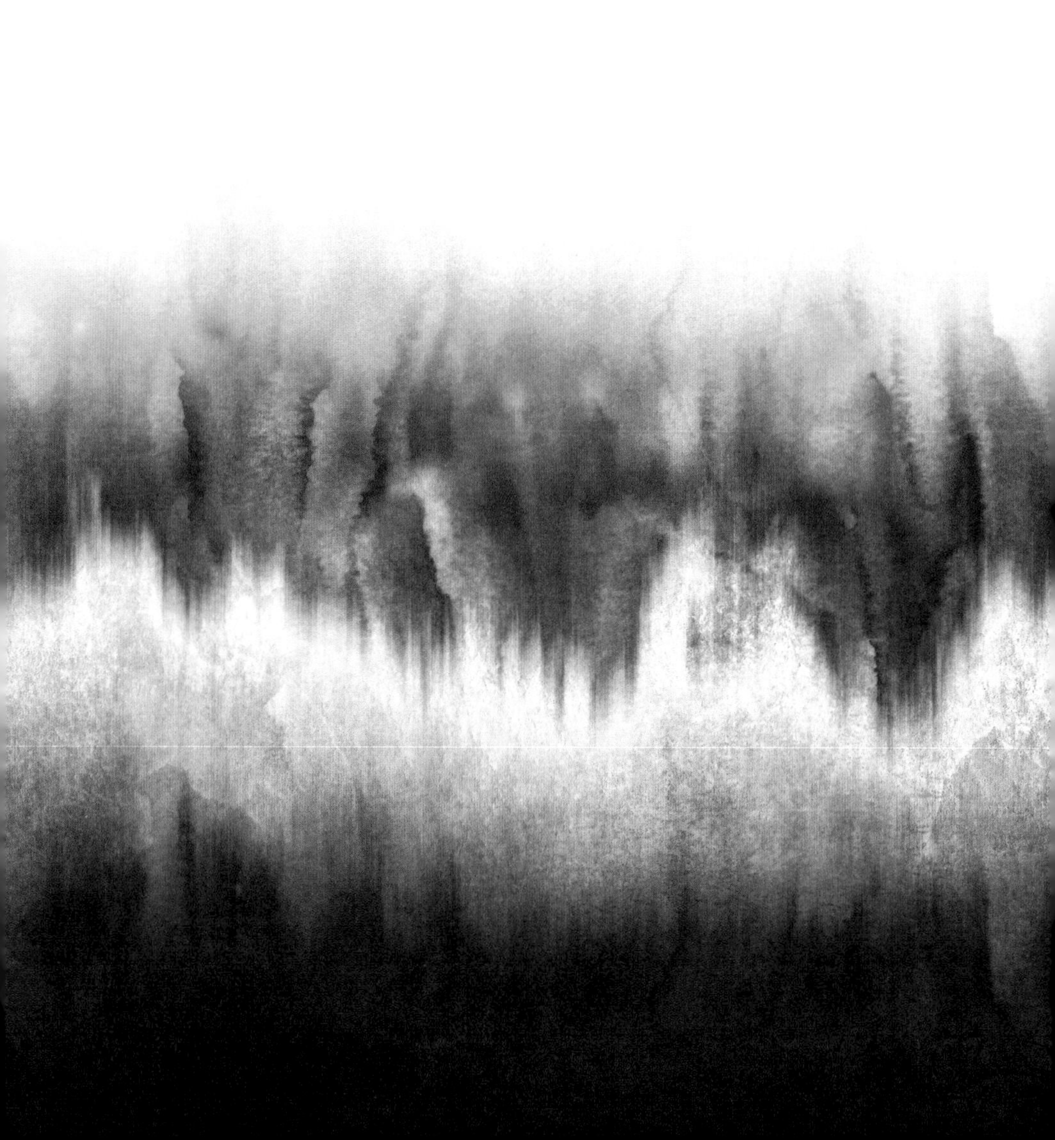

BREATHE

So here you are at last, among the trees.

Whether you are in a city park, town trail system, state forest, national park, or private woodland; whether the acreage you stand on is large or small; whether the trees are towering old giants or young upstarts; whether you can hear traffic nearby or not; whether you are with others or alone; whether it is hot or cold, rainy or sunny or snowing; whether you are in shape or not; whether you know anything about trees and wildlife or not . . . you are here.

you
are
here

pause

Before you enter the woods, before you take another step, take a moment to scan your body and mind.

Take a slow, deep breath.

Then, begin with your toes. Wiggle them. Feel the soles of your feet pressing against the ground.

Work your way up your body, letting your attention rest a moment on each part of you, noting where you feel tightness, tension, or stress. When you do, pause to take a few extra breaths. Imagine your muscles relaxing with each exhale.

Unclench your hands.

Bring your shoulders up to your ears, and then let them drop. Imagine a weight dropping with them, falling down your arms and flowing off your fingertips.

What sort of chatter is running through your head?

Tell yourself you are going to focus on something else now. For a moment, just listen to yourself breathe.

Put your hand on your belly and begin your breath there. Feel your chest expand and contract.

Visualize your lungs inside your ribcage, filling with fresh air. Your lungs are filling with the breath of trees.

As the trees
breathe out,
you breathe in;

as the trees
breathe in,

you
breathe
out.

In some mysterious way, woods have never seemed to me to be static things. In physical terms, I move through them; yet in metaphysical ones, they seem to move through me.

—John Fowles

open
up

Trees "breathe in" carbon dioxide and release oxygen and water vapor through tiny holes in their leaves called stomata, a word that comes from the Greek word meaning "mouth." On 1 square millimeter of a leaf, there are 100 to 1,000 of these little mouths, all breathing. One mature tree breathes in 48 pounds of carbon dioxide each year — and the exhalations of two mature trees provide enough oxygen for you to breathe for more than a year.

As you stand beneath the trees and breathe, imagine your own pores softening and opening, making you more permeable to the natural world around you.

All things share the same breath — the beast, the tree, the man . . . the air shares its spirit with all the life it supports.

— *Chief Seattle*

sit
still

When you first enter the woods, it may seem still and silent, save for the birds or few creatures who startle ahead of you, warning others of your presence. Enter the woods quietly, in a posture of gratitude, and you will be a little less disruptive.

Sit as still as you can in one place for a while —

20 minutes or so — and see how the forest begins to slowly go about its business again all around you.

Why did this spring wood
Grow so silent when I came?
What was happening?

—*Richard Wright*

Richard Wright, author of *Native Son* and *Black Boy*, wrote more than 4,000 haiku in the final 18 months of his life. With their strict syllable counts and evocative images of nature, these haiku, according to Wright's daughter Julia, were

"self-developed antidotes against illness."

At his home in Hawaii, poet W. S. Merwin turned 19 acres of decimated land — formerly a pineapple plantation — into a lush palm forest, one hand-planted seedling at a time. Now, the Merwin Palm Collection has over 2,740 individual palm trees, representing more than 400 species. It is one of the largest palm collections on earth. Where once the wind moved over a wasteland, now it moves through myriad rustling palm fronds. In his poem "Place," Merwin writes:

> On the last day of the world
> I would want to plant a tree.

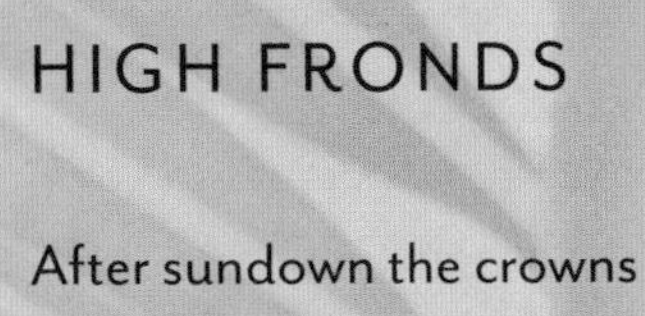

HIGH FRONDS

After sundown the crowns
of the tallest palms
stand out against
the clear glass of the eastern sky
they have no shadows
and no memory
the wind has gone its own way
nothing is missing

—W. S. Merwin

step
softly

Vietnamese Buddhist monk Thich Nhat Hanh teaches "walking meditation," an intentional way of being mindful and present as you walk. Focus on your breath and repeat a phrase in your mind. You can choose your own words or images to focus on as you walk. Perhaps you breathe in and think of being rooted, like a tree; breathe out and think of being light, like a leaf in the wind.

Breathe in and think,
I am solid;
breathe out and think,
I am free.

With each step the earth heals us, and with each step we heal the earth.

— Thich Nhat Hanh

Deer Park Monastery is a mindfulness practice center and monastic training center established by Zen Master Thich Nhat Hanh. Surrounded by oak trees, the monastery is located on a 400-acre preserve in the chaparral mountains of southern California. At right is an excerpt from Tess Gallagher's poem "Walking Meditation with Thich Nhat Hanh."

Fifty of us follow him loosely
up the mountain at Deer Park Monastery.
We are in the slow motion of a dream
lifting off the dreamer's brow. Steps
into steps and the body rising out
of them like smoke from a fire
with many legs. Gradually the flames
die down and the earth is finally under us.
Inside the mountain a centipede crawls
into no-up, no-down.

— *Tess Gallagher*

turn
to the
wind

Turn now from your own breath, from the trees' breath, to the breath of the wind — the little puffs and eddies, heaving storms and flowing currents that move in the ocean of our atmosphere.

What does the wind carry with it today?

A change in the weather?

A bit of sweetness, or a wet chill?

A puff of cottonwood seed,

a swirl of dust,

laughter from a nearby playground . . . ?

The trees are tickled and played by the wind, buffeted and broken and uprooted by the wind, even shaped by the wind. In exposed, blustery places such as rocky mountaintops and seashores, you may be able to tell the direction the wind usually blows by looking at the trees, especially conifers. Their branches look like they are streaming in one direction — downwind. This is called "flagging."

psithurism

the sound of wind in the trees and rustling of leaves

Gerard Manley Hopkins was one of the greatest poets of the Victorian era. Though he was a Jesuit priest, he is known as a nature writer as much as a religious writer. His keen observations of the natural world are brought to life in language so rich and textured that his poems leap into both physical and spiritual ecstasy. Here he is on the intimacy of air.

Wild air, world-mothering air,
Nestling me everywhere,
That each eyelash or hair
Girdles; goes home betwixt
The fleeciest, frailest-flixed
Snowflake; that's fairly mixed
With riddles, and is rife
In every least thing's life;
This needful, never spent,
And nursing element;
My more than meat and drink,
My meal at every wink;
This air, which, by life's law,
My lung must draw and draw
Now but to breathe its praise . . .

— Gerard Manley Hopkins

On mountaintops and subarctic landscapes, trees that endure the cold, fierce winds become gnarled and stunted. These scrubby survivors are called *krummholz,* a German word meaning "crooked, bent, twisted." And though they are small, they may also be quite ancient.

Such trees — such people, too — have stories to tell.

This musical excerpt is from *Krummholz Variations,* a musical tone poem for flute, clarinet, two bassoons, two trumpets, and two trombones. Twisted krummholz serve as gateways to the alpine zone and as mountaintop sentinels. I treasure them for their unique deformities. High altitude landscapes are a paradigm for beauty in the face of harshness. When times are tough, I find hope in moments of joy and serenity that blossom amidst extremes. They remind me of the human spirit and our great capacity for resilience, a new possibility in every breath.

— Oliver Caplan, composer

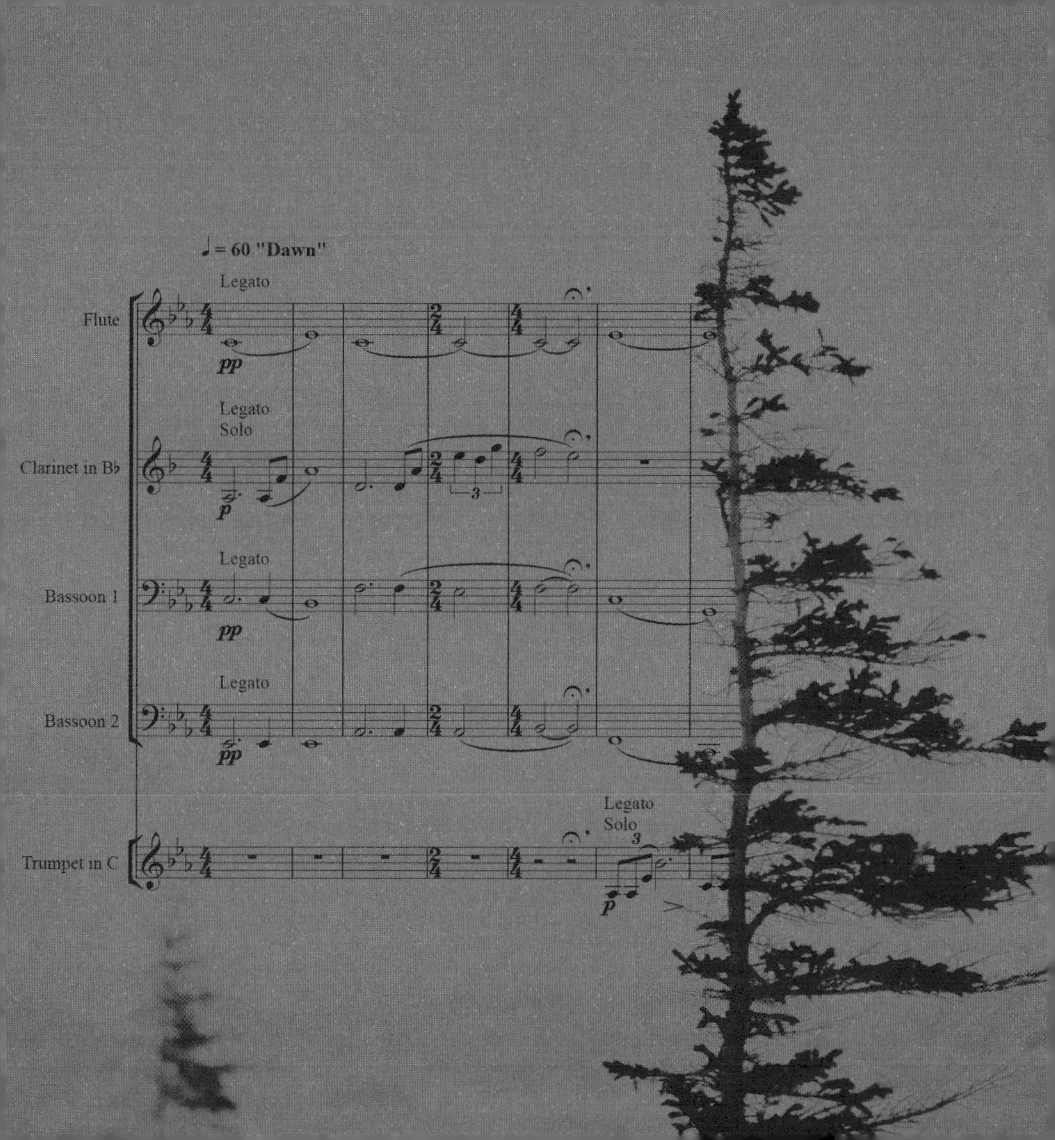
♩= 60 "Dawn"
Legato
Flute
pp
Legato
Solo
Clarinet in B♭
p
3
Legato
Bassoon 1
pp
Legato
Bassoon 2
pp
Legato
Solo
Trumpet in C
3
p

Naturalist, conservationist, and writer John Muir (1838–1914) was an early and passionate voice in the movement to preserve wilderness in the United States. Often called the "Father of the National Parks," Muir co-founded the Sierra Club and petitioned Congress for a bill that resulted in the creation of Yosemite National Park. As a writer, he has deeply influenced the way Americans see their wild lands. He advised,

"Keep close to Nature's heart . . . and break clear away, once in awhile, and climb a mountain or spend a week in the woods. Wash your spirit clean."

The winds go to every tree, fingering every leaf and branch and furrowed bole; not one is forgotten; the Mountain Pine towering with outstretched arms on the rugged buttresses of the icy peaks, the lowliest and most retiring tenant of the dells; they seek and find them all, caressing them tenderly, bending them in lusty exercise, stimulating their growth, plucking off a leaf or limb as required, or removing an entire tree or grove, now whispering and cooing through the branches like a sleepy child, now roaring like the ocean.

—*John Muir*

It was the wind that gave them life. It is the wind that comes out of our mouths now that gives us life. When this ceases to blow we die. In the skin at the tips of our fingers we see the trail of the wind, it shows us the wind blew when our ancestors were created.

— *Navajo saying*

The wind has been revered as sacred for centuries and across many cultures,

from Native Americans to the ancient Greeks.

In Greek, the words *breath*, *wind*, and *spirit* are all the same: *pneuma*.

And in Hebrew, the word for all three is *ruach*.

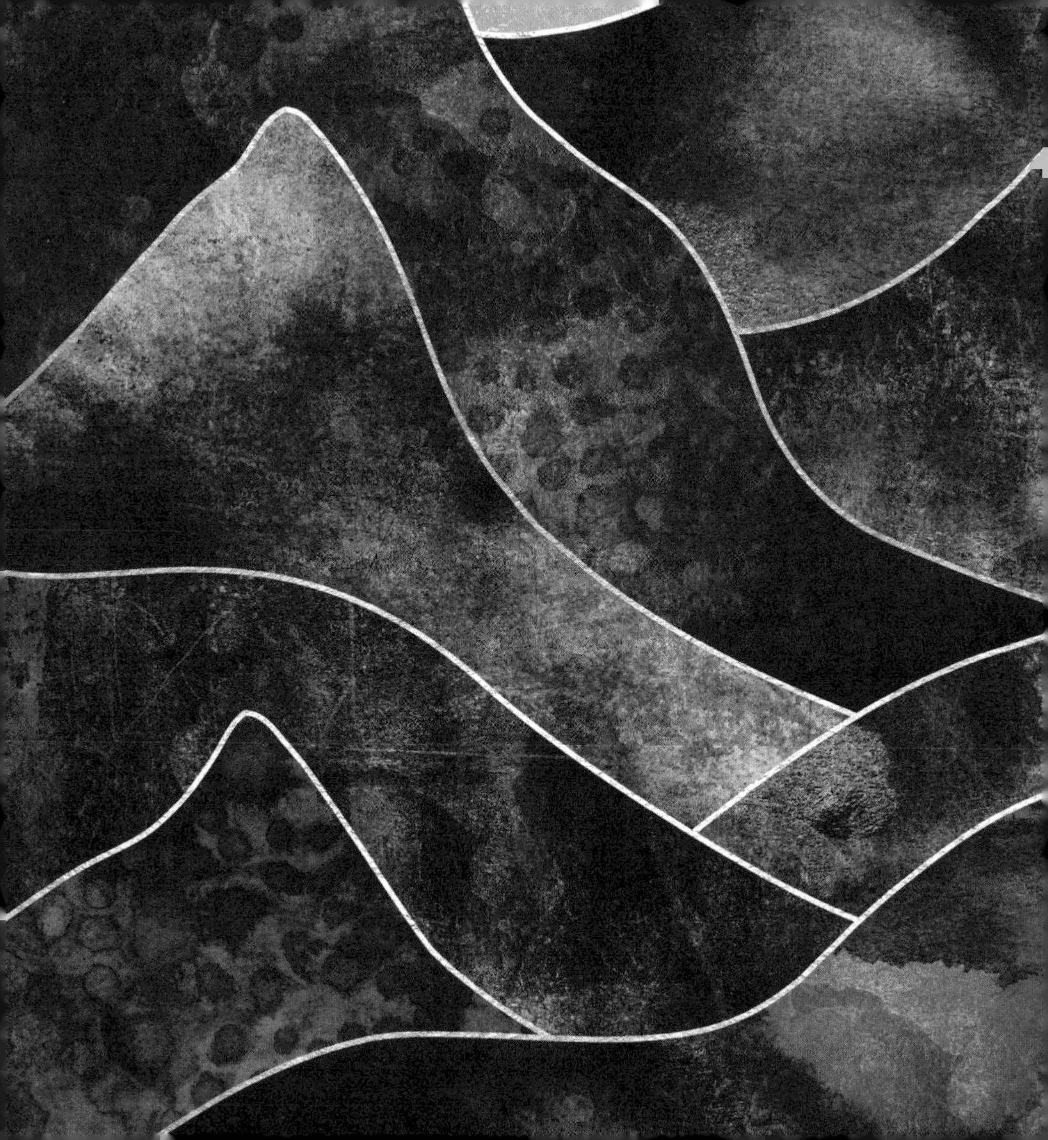

CONNECT

The roots of a tree are a vast network, branching and rebranching, finding their way through the soil and around rocks, taking in nutrients, connecting the tree to the earth, to other trees, and to the various living things that reside in the darkness underground — insects, bacteria, fungi, and burrowing creatures. Aboveground, branches grow toward the light, crisscrossing the sky, bending in the wind.

In ways completely foreign to us,

trees sense the world around them,

reacting and adapting to changes in their environment, and even communicating with each other.

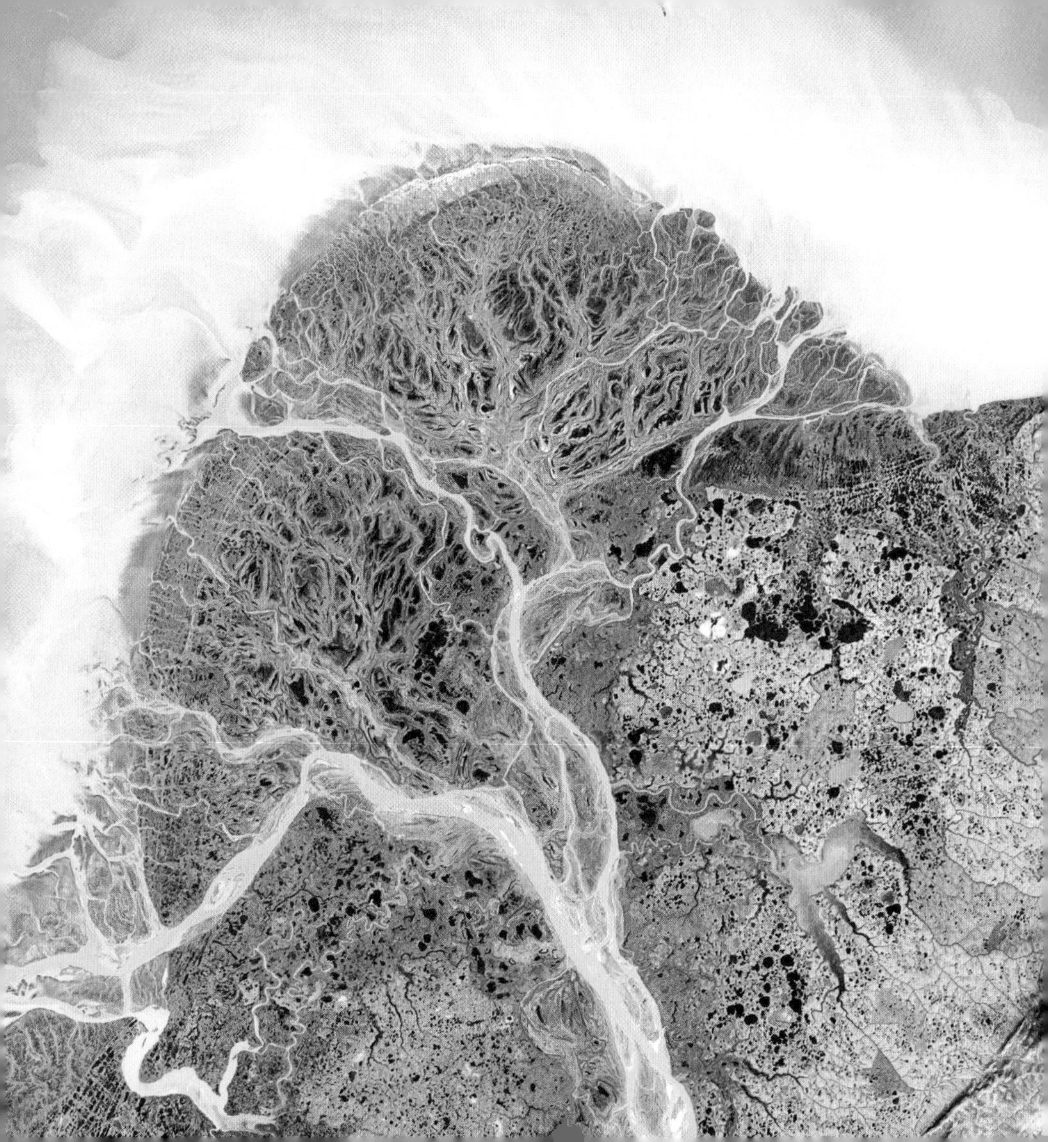

In these maple and birch and beech the branches reach out year after year, running skyward like the fingers of rivulets when water is poured on dry ground. Water is at the heart of their form; they have the shape of river systems seen from space, or veins of blood, or nerves. Standing there, buds swollen, with a wash of deep red over them, they seem as lambent and as alive and as ready as anything on earth could be.

— *Diana Kappel-Smith*

reach
out

Now that you have found your center —
your own breath — and let the forest puff its
green breath across your skin,
it is time to turn further outward,
to send out your tendrils and roots and
search for connection.

As you walk through
the forest,
feel your own body
react and respond.
Invite the forest in
through your senses . . .

look

Pretend you have just been granted the gift of sight. Instead of looking *at* things,

look
for
things.

Play a game of noticing. Seek out small details that might otherwise escape your attention. Take delight in discovering:

Patterns in bark
Delicate plants
growing close to
the ground
The intricate
shapes that
ice makes
Bursts of lichen
on rocks

We step from darkly clustered spruce
into birch — pink and white,
bark peeled into sunrise like sloughed skin.
And though it is raining,
it is as if a shattered sun, golden leaves,
falls in shards through the gray
October sky to glow around us.

— *Hannah Fries*

komorebi
(Japanese)
sunlight filtering through
the leaves of trees

listen

Get your other senses working now.

Stop walking, close your eyes, and listen.

You are not in a hurry.

Do you hear rustling leaves or the creak of
branches rubbing together?
Birds? Scurrying animals? Trickling water?

If it is very cold, you might hear popping sounds
as trees' sap freezes, creating frost cracks.

As you listen, try to separate
the layers of sound in your mind.
Follow them to their sources.

THE SOUND OF TREES

I wonder about the trees:
Why do we wish to bear
Forever the noise of these
More than another noise
So close to our dwelling place?
We suffer them by the day
Till we lose all measure of pace
And fixity in our joys,
And acquire a listening air.
They are that that talks of going
But never gets away;
And that talks no less for knowing,
As it grows wiser and older,
That now it means to stay.

My feet tug at the floor
And my head sways to my shoulder
Sometimes when I watch trees sway
From the window or the door.
I shall set forth for somewhere,
I shall make the reckless choice,
Some day when they are in voice
And tossing so as to scare
The white clouds over them on.
I shall have less to say,
But I shall be gone.

—Robert Frost

Composer Jean Sibelius was deeply influenced by the natural world. His op. 75 consists of five pieces named for trees in his native Finland: rowan, pine, aspen, birch, and spruce. Writing in the *New Yorker,* Alex Ross noted that "instead of writing the music of his imagination, [Sibelius] wanted to transcribe the very noise of nature. He thought that he could hear chords in the murmurs of the forests and the lapping of the lakes; he once baffled a group of Finnish students by giving a lecture on the overtone series of a meadow."

smell

Have you ever said that the air smells "like fall" or "like spring"?

What are you smelling?

Dry leaves? Honeysuckle?

Thawing snow?

Wet earth and fresh green leaves?

Get closer.

Scratch a twig with your nail and smell the damp wood beneath.

Crush a leaf of wintergreen and hold it to your nose.

I discovered a whole assortment of tree scents. On hot, dry summer days, the balsams, spruces, and pines acted like giant sticks of incense, giving off a redolence which filled the air inside and outside the cabin. The carpet of dead needles, the dry duff, the trickles of pitch, the sun-warmed bark itself, all gave off subtle odors. The live needles tanged the air with what old-time doctors called "balsamifers."

—*Anne LaBastille*

petrichor
the smell of earth after rain

touch

The forest is full of textures — the soft fronds of ferns or mosses, the smooth bark of a birch or rough bark of a pine, an ice-cold stream, a slick stone. What does the ground feel like beneath your feet? Hard and rocky? Soft and needle-strewn? Perhaps you feel some mud suck at a shoe. Perhaps you take your shoes off — let your feet get in contact with the ground beneath them, skin to earth.

Get a little risky. Nature is nothing if not sensual.

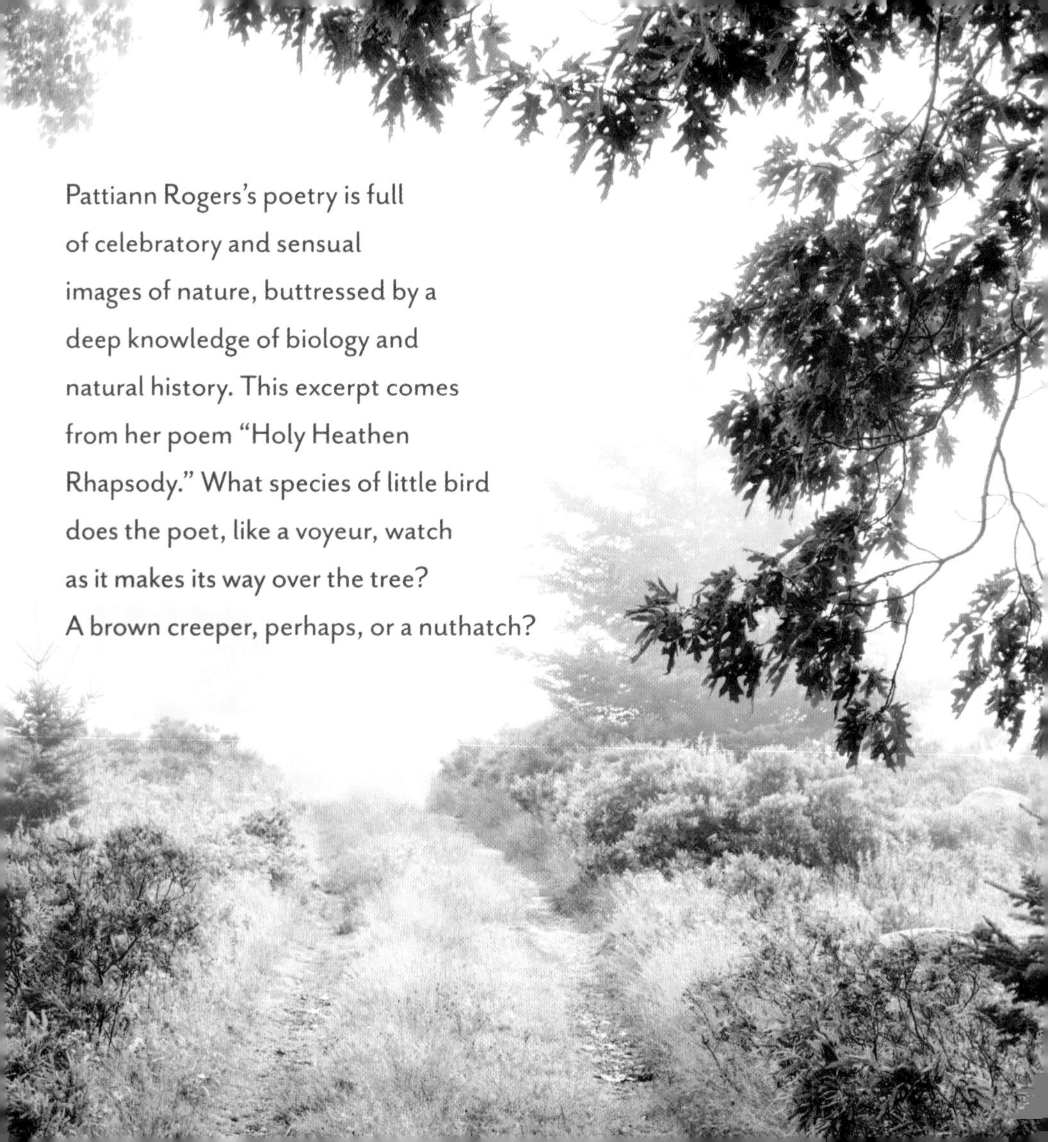

Pattiann Rogers's poetry is full of celebratory and sensual images of nature, buttressed by a deep knowledge of biology and natural history. This excerpt comes from her poem "Holy Heathen Rhapsody." What species of little bird does the poet, like a voyeur, watch as it makes its way over the tree? A brown creeper, perhaps, or a nuthatch?

Summer lolls, lingers in its own mazes,
a white-limbed poplar, leafstalks, peel
of scented bark. Her body — seed wing
or feather down, thread slivers of silk —
touches each curled love and creviced branch
as she passes, slides underside, overside,
along the ridges and furrows. (Is that a tiny
tongue finding the way?) Love is this sun-
holding tree of lapping leaves, delves,
canopies, a multi-tangled cover.

— *Pattiann Rogers*

taste if you dare

If you know what you've found is wild blueberry or blackberry. If a broken sugar maple bough is dripping sap. If you like the sour pucker of wood sorrel. Or just taste the air — the senses of smell and taste are closely connected. If you are near the ocean, you might detect salt on the breeze. If you are in a pine forest, you might feel as though you can taste the sun-warmed resin. If it is raining or snowing,

stick out your tongue.

Sugar maple, we say, and it is on our tongues:
Tap it now, in March,
the ground a mash of snow and mud, sap rising
from the roots, a clear drop on the finger:
small sweetness we taste because we know it's there.

— Hannah Fries

be seen

Now pause and look at the trees again,

at the plants and birds, squirrels and insects, and other living things around you. Remember that you are not the only one doing the sensing. You are being heard, seen, felt — sensed in ways you cannot understand.

As the crickets' soft autumn hum

is to us

so are we to the trees

as are they

to the rocks and the hills.

—*Gary Snyder*

marvel

Did you know that trees can "hear"?
Scientists found that plants' roots
will grow toward the sound of water.

But the plants are not fools:

They not only grew toward running water,
but also grew away from sounds they did not like.
If there was already enough water in the
surrounding soil, however, the plants did not
respond to the sound of water.

It was surprising and extraordinary to see that the plant could actually tell when the sound of running water was a recording and when it was real, and that the plant did not like the recorded sound.

— Monica Gagliano, research associate professor in evolutionary ecology, University of Western Australia

---

It may be that plants have more complex senses than we have yet to imagine.

One of the ways in which trees "talk" is in the form of electrical pulses via a system of voltage-based signaling not unlike animals' nervous systems.

The forest is crackling with secret conversation.

Poet and Trappist monk Thomas Merton wrote,
"I live in the woods out of necessity.
I get out of bed in the middle of the night
because it is imperative that I hear the
silence of the night, alone, and,
with my face on the floor, say psalms, alone,
in the silence of the night."

What a thing it is to sit absolutely alone,
in the forest, at night, cherished by this
wonderful, unintelligible,
perfectly innocent speech,
the most comforting speech in the world,
the talk that rain makes by itself all over the ridges,
and the talk of the watercourses everywhere in the hollows!
Nobody started it, nobody is going to stop it.
It will talk as long as it wants, this rain.
As long as it talks I am going to listen.

— *Thomas Merton*

Trees and plants also stay in touch via a vast network of fungi whose thin, branching threads of mycelia grow among their roots and throughout the forest soil. Through this network, trees share and exchange nutrients. Older trees may actually help younger trees survive. They can even warn each other of harmful fungi and diseases by sending chemical signals through the delicate filaments of mycelia.

Yes, trees are the foundation of forests, but a forest is much more than what you see. . . . Underground there is this other world, a world of infinite biological pathways that connect trees and allow them to communicate and allow the forest to behave as though it's a single organism. It might remind you of a sort of intelligence.

— Suzanne Simard, forest ecologist,
University of British Columbia

dendrophile

someone who loves trees and forests

As you take in the trees and
all the life that revolves around them,
as you begin to sense their intelligence,
as you breathe their breath and
touch their bark and listen to their
clacking branches, you might
start to feel the boundaries between
you and them grow softer.

Let it happen.

The mountains, I become part of it . . .

The herbs, the fir tree, I become part of it.

The morning mists, the clouds, the gathering waters,

I become part of it.

The wilderness, the dew drops, the pollen . . .

I become part of it.

—Navajo chant

As you watch
a tree sway in wind,
let your knees and
shoulders relax.
Sway a little on your
own stem.

Everything I encounter permeates me,
washes in and out, leaving a tracery,
placing me in that beautiful paradox of being
by which I am both a solitary creature and
everyone, everything.

— *Susan Griffin*

Let your imagination leap into another body.

The body of a beetle.

The body of a tree. What do you feel?

I sense the branches moving, feel the creak of winter stiffness, feel new life begin to run through its body as the sun and wind pull and push. I feel the pull on kinky limbs, the sluggishness of parts still half asleep that respond only slowly to the call of the sun. I feel the breeze blow off the tree's winter coat and awaken something inside, deep within the core. And I sense the tree responding, branches swaying, bulky body moving slowly, sluggishly, as it can.

And then I *am* the tree. [A] jay alights and I feel its touch as on a distant extremity. I am still here, still flat on the hillside hidden from the wind, but somehow I extend above and beyond and around myself to include the tree, the earth, the rocks, the breeze.

— *Barbara Dean*

root
your
spirit

Once you become practiced at being more physically connected to the world through your senses, you will likely find that something deeper inside you is reaching out for connection, too.

Perhaps this is partly because your growing awareness causes you also to recognize your smallness.

Your spirit, looking to re-root itself, sends out its feelers into the largeness of the world.

TREE

It is foolish
to let a young redwood
grow next to a house.
Even in this
one lifetime,
you will have to choose.
That great calm being,
this clutter of soup pots and books —
Already the first branch-tips brush at the window.
Softly, calmly, immensity taps at your life.

—Jane Hirshfield

It is an ongoing journey, this reaching out, and out again. And the universe, with all of its patterns and chaos and myriad threads of connection, is both terrifying and wondrous. Take a page from the trees:

focus on being both rooted in the earth and searching among the stars.

find
harmony

If you look closely at the natural world, you may begin to see patterns amid what seems like chaos — unexpected connections thrumming everywhere around us.

Time and time again I am astounded by the regularity and repetition of form . . . basic patterns, sculpted by time and the land, appearing everywhere I look. The twisted branches in the forest that look so much like the forked antlers of the deer and elk. The way the glacier-polished hillside boulders look like the muscular, rounded bodies of the animals — deer, bear — that pass among these boulders like loving ghosts. The way the swirling deer hair is the exact shape and size of the larch and pine needles the deer hair lies upon once it is torn loose and comes to rest on the forest floor.

— *Rick Bass*

How many spiral patterns can you find as you walk through the woods?

The "golden ratio," or Fibonacci sequence, is a cosmic code: the sum of the first two numbers equals the third number, the sum of the second and third equals the fourth, and so on. As the numbers grow, the ratio between any number and the one previous approaches 1.618.

In gorgeous evidence of the organization of nature, this pattern can be seen in the spirals of a pinecone, the inner ear, a nautilus shell, a hurricane, or a galaxy.

The pines glittered with their innumerable green needles in the light, and seemed to challenge me to read their riddle. The drab oak-leaves of the last year turned their little somersets and lay still again. And the wind bustled high overhead in the forest top. This gay and grand architecture, from the vault to the moss and lichen on which I lay, — who shall explain to me the laws of its proportions and adornments?

— *Ralph Waldo Emerson*

HEAL

Some days, some weeks, maybe even some months, it is easy to feel like a broken tree after an ice storm: full of cracked branches creaking in their cases of ice.

Simple acts of connection — with a landscape, with animals, or with other people — can go a long way in helping us feel whole again, both physically and emotionally.

After all, humans are social animals; we depend on our communities to survive, and that includes our ecological community. The air we breathe, the water we drink, the soil and sun that feed us — we cannot truly disconnect ourselves from any of it any more than a tree can.

And yet, within our busy indoor existence, we come to feel isolated and alienated. The weight of the world is heavy indeed. The weight of our own lives can be heavy at times, too. But it is heavier when we stay inside our sealed boxes, the pressure bearing in from all sides.

When you step outdoors and under a canopy of trees, when you give yourself time to breathe, time to get to know the trees and their world, you feel that pressure lift and dissipate.

release

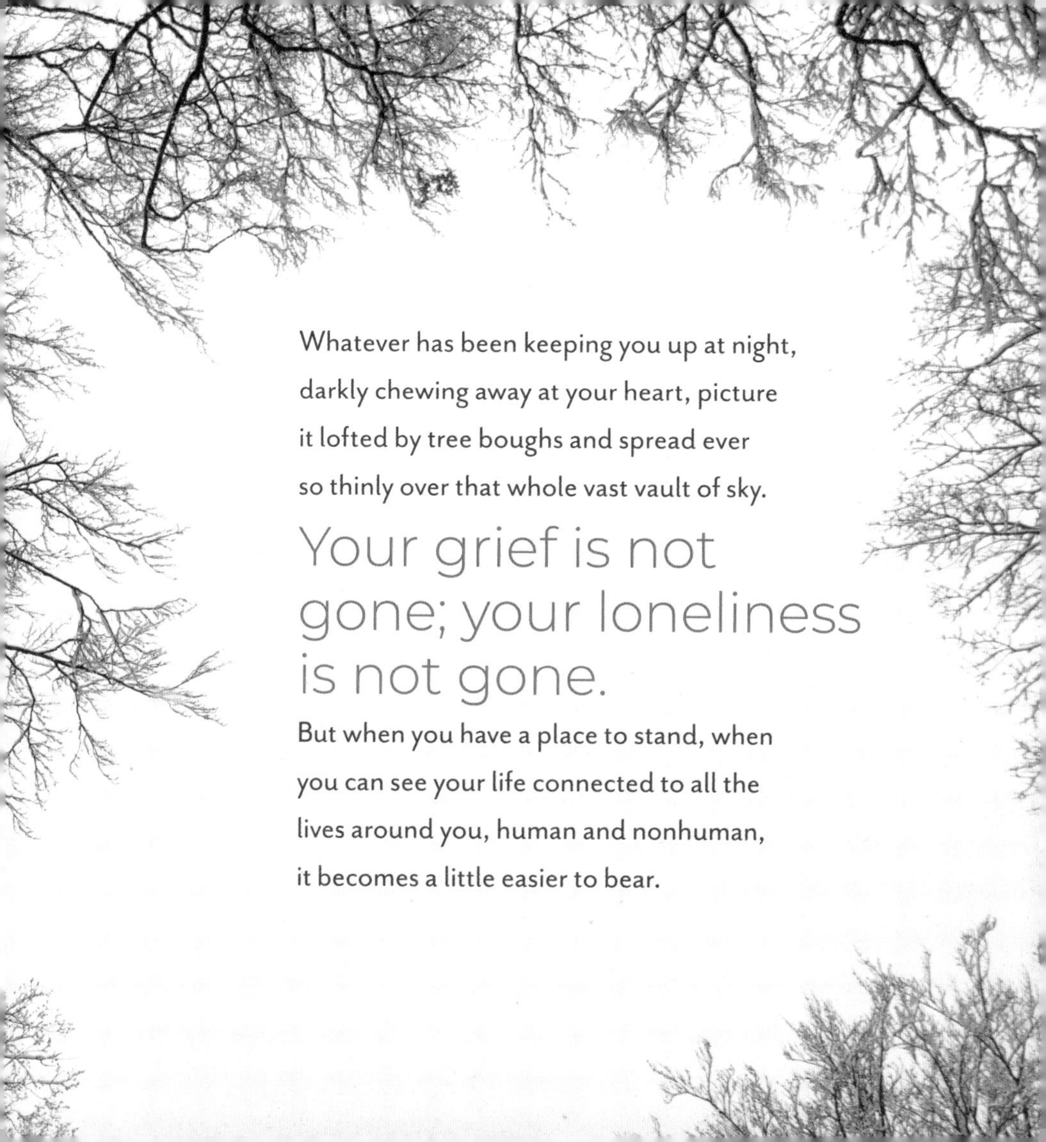

Whatever has been keeping you up at night, darkly chewing away at your heart, picture it lofted by tree boughs and spread ever so thinly over that whole vast vault of sky.

Your grief is not gone; your loneliness is not gone.

But when you have a place to stand, when you can see your life connected to all the lives around you, human and nonhuman, it becomes a little easier to bear.

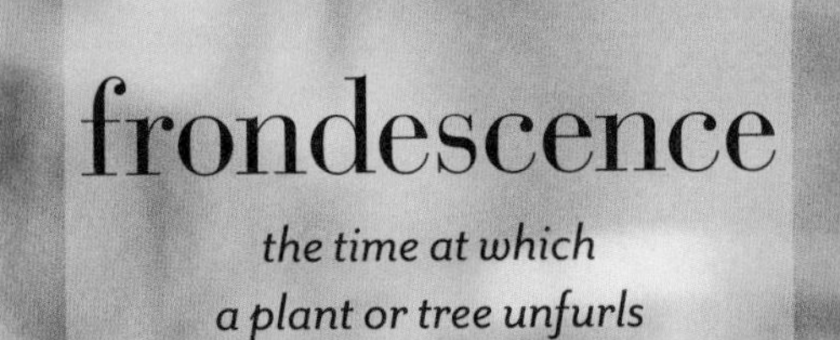

frondescence

the time at which
a plant or tree unfurls
its leaves

ON THE MOUNTAIN: A CONVERSATION

You ask

why I perch

on a jade green mountain?

I laugh

but say nothing

my heart

free

like a peach blossom

in the flowing stream

going by

in the depths

in another world

not among men.

—*Li Po*

The trees' medicine is our medicine, too.

The feeling of well-being we get from spending time in the woods is more than psychological. Trees release antimicrobial chemicals into the air called phytoncides to help defend themselves against harmful insects and germs. These chemicals are closely related to essential oils. That wonderfully intoxicating scent of cedar, for example, is the result of phytoncides.

When we breathe the forest air, phytoncides stimulate our "natural killer cells," white blood cells in our bodies that attack tumors and viruses. So, when you walk among the trees, your immune system gets a boost from the trees' own medicine.

The woods, the trees,
and the rocks give man
the resonance he needs.
— Ludwig van Beethoven

soothe

Walking among the trees calms the brain and the nerves, but even only a glimpse of the treetops can help. Hospital patients who can see trees from their windows heal faster, need less pain medication, and have fewer complications. And yes, being among the trees can lower your blood pressure,

but those of us who have been there know that trees are just good for the heart.

I think that I cannot preserve my health and spirits, unless I spend four hours a day at least — and it is commonly more than that — sauntering through the woods and over the hills and fields, absolutely free from all worldly engagements.

— Henry David Thoreau

solivagant
wandering alone

Every wound ever suffered
remains within a tree,
but while they may not heal,
most trees do get closure.

*—Michael Snyder, forester,
commissioner of the Vermont Department
of Forests, Parks, and Recreation*

The way trees heal their wounds is quite different from how the human body heals, though perhaps not so different from how the human psyche heals. First, the wood around the wound goes through a chemical change to make the area inhospitable to bacteria and fungi that would begin the process of decay. Then the tree seals off the wound with a special kind of wood called "callus." The injured part of the tree does not go away, but it stays contained, and new growth is able to form around it.

What wounds do you carry within you?

Have you grown around and past them yet, or are they still threatening to spread and decay?

bend,
don't
break

When you feel heavy, in danger of being crushed, try to think of yourself as more flexible and less brittle.

Evergreen boughs sagging under the snow
are strong because they bend, beautiful because
they hold all that luminous weight without snapping.
And they bounce again skyward come spring.

My help is in the mountain
Where I take myself to heal
The earthly wounds
That people give to me.
I find a rock with sun on it
And a stream where the water runs gentle
And the trees which one by one
give me company.
So must I stay for a long time
Until I have grown from the rock
And the stream is running through me
And I cannot tell myself from one tall tree.
Then I know that nothing touches me
Nor makes me run away.
My help is in the mountain
That I take away with me.

— *Nancy Wood*

find lightness

On a branch
floating downriver
a cricket, singing.
— *Kobayashi Issa*

Perhaps it is not only the boxes of our homes and offices that trap us sometimes, weighing us down, but also our egos.

When we find ourselves amid something much larger than ourselves — larger even than all the intricate machinations of the society in which we live — a certain lightness takes over. But it is a lightness filled with the freedom of losing oneself, and the strength of finding oneself again, humbly.

ESCAPE

When we get out of the glass bottles of our ego,
and when we escape like squirrels turning in the cages of our personality
and get into the forests again,
we shall shiver with cold and fright
but things will happen to us
so that we don't know ourselves.
Cool, unlying life will rush in,
and passion will make our bodies taut with power,
we shall stamp our feet with new power,
and old things will fall down,
we shall laugh, and institutions will curl up like burnt paper.

—*D. H. Lawrence*

celebrate renewal

Feeling more alive and connected, paradoxically, can help soothe the fear of death that grips us sometimes like a disease. And seeing the way nature continually dies and renews itself, decays and is reborn, can help slowly round the sharp edges of grief.

Observe the cycles of life and death around you. Look for evidence.

Fallen leaves
decaying on the
forest floor as
new leaves
bud out above
A rotten log
teeming with
insect life, fungi,
and moss
New shoots
growing out
of a stump
The carcass
of an animal
melting into
the soil

When a tree falls and begins to decay, new seedlings take root on the back of the old trunk. Moss and other plants take hold in the soft crevices that fill with nutrient-rich soil, and many small animals make their homes here.

These fallen trees, nurturers even in death, are called "nurse logs."

Birth, life and death—
each took place on the
hidden side of a leaf.
—*Toni Morrison*

A WALK IN MARCH

This hill
crossed with broken pines and maples
lumpy with the burial mounds of
uprooted hemlocks (hurricane
of '38) out of their
rotting hearts generations rise
trying once more to become
the forest
just beyond them
tall enough to be called trees
in their youth like aspen a bouquet
of young beech is gathered
they still wear last summer's leaves

the lightest brown almost translucent
how their stubbornness has decorated
the winter woods
on this narrow path ice tries
to keep the black undecaying oak leaves
in its crackling grip   it's become
too hard to walk   at last a
sunny patch   oh!   i'm in water
to my ankles   APRIL

—*Grace Paley*

At 5,062 years old, a bristlecone pine in the White Mountains of California is the oldest living tree in the world.

In the Pacific Northwest, there are pockets of old-growth forest where Douglas fir trees have grown to be as old as 750 years; they can be 6 feet in diameter and over 250 feet tall.

Think of an old giant tree in the forest, where humans have not interfered for a long, long time, where the moss creeps intricately at its own pace and the forest floor is made of many layers of rich decay.

Imagine what time might feel like to a tree.

Not linear, but cyclic,

defined not by minutes and seconds, but centuries,

beholden to the present as much as the past and future.

waldeinsamkeit

(German)

the feeling of being alone in the woods

I drink old-growth forest in like water. This is the homeland that built us. Here I walk shoulder to shoulder with history — my history. I am in the presence of something ancient and venerable, perhaps of time itself, its unhurried passing marked by immensity and stolidity, each year purged by fire cinched by a ring. Here mortality's roving hands grapple with air. I can see my place as human in a natural order more grand, whole, and functional than I've ever witnessed, and I am humbled, not frightened by it. Comforted. It is as if a round table springs up in the cathedral of pines and God graciously pulls out a chair for me, and I no longer have to worry about what happens to souls.

—Janisse Ray

GIVE

THANKS

Picture the shape of an elm tree:

like a vase gracefully opening toward the sky.
Or like a person, head back, arms flung up in joy and gratitude.

As you get to know the trees and the natural world that surrounds you, it seems that the more you open yourself to receive, the more you are given.

Breathe the loamy, rich scent of the woods, and feel renewed.
Begin to recognize the texture of different kinds bark, and feel joy.
Examine the veins of a leaf and consider the lines on your own hands.
Hear the clacking of branches above, and it sounds like music you'd forgotten.

You breathe again, take another step forward, and feel peace.

Something mysterious and familiar wells up from deep in the pit of your belly, rises to your chest, begins to flow through your limbs.

The gifts we receive from being in the presence of trees are pure grace.

Certainly, we have done nothing to deserve them. Considering the destruction humankind has wrought on nature, we may not want to think about what we "deserve."

And yet, an embarrassment of riches has been set before us. What can we do but give thanks — to nature, to God, to whatever you call the larger force you feel moving in the world.

grace

i thank You God for most this amazing
day: for the leaping greenly spirits of trees
and a blue true dream of sky; and for everything
which is natural which is infinite which is yes
(i who have died am alive again today,
and this is the sun's birthday; this is the birth
day of life and of love and wings: and of the gay
great happening illimitably earth)
how should tasting touching hearing seeing
breathing any — lifted from the no
of all nothing — human merely being
doubt unimaginable You?
(now the ears of my ears awake and
now the eyes of my eyes are opened)

— e. e. cummings

Gratitude often comes on the heels of wonder. Perhaps wonder itself is, at times, an involuntary expression of gratitude. Spend enough time letting yourself be porous to the world, and letting your curiosity lead you, and wonder will find you frequently. So frequently, in fact, that you will not be surprised to feel it welling up again and again. You will come to depend on it.

What, if only the tiniest thing, astonished you today?

What a strange thing!
to be alive
beneath cherry blossoms.

—Kobayashi Issa

Lord make us mindful of the
little things that grow and blossom
in these days to make the world
beautiful for us.

—W. E. B. Du Bois

If you look at a tree and think of it as a design assignment, it would be like asking you to make something that makes oxygen, sequesters carbon, fixes nitrogen, distills water, provides habitat for hundreds of species, accrues solar energy's fuel, makes complex sugars and food, changes colors with the seasons, creates microclimates, and self-replicates.

— William McDonough, architect and designer

Some of the oldest and most massive living organisms in the world are groves of quaking aspen. These groves look like individual trees but are actually all part of the same enormous clone and share a common root system. The oldest one that we know of spans 107 acres and is made up of approximately 47,000 genetically identical trees. This clone, which lives in Utah, has a name — Pando, the Trembling Giant — and it is thought to be about 80,000 years old. Pando took root long before the first humans arrived in North America.

Astonishment is the
only proper response.

— *David George Haskell*

invite enchantment

Allow yourself to feel ecstatic, to celebrate and sing the praises of all the small (and large) things that bring you joy. Cynicism might be hip — and it might feel safer to be emotionally guarded — but it also might stifle the soul. Practice being openly enchanted by the world.

Now and then, point out the beautiful and curious things around you to friends and family, perhaps even to strangers. Your enchantment will give others permission to be enchanted, too. You might be amazed how few people notice the enormous sycamore that grows right in front of the downtown McDonald's, its white bark and wide-spreading limbs stark against the sky.

You are hardwired for wonder: let your soul leap.

Poet Edna St. Vincent Millay grew up on the coast of Maine but spent the last half of her life, from 1925 to 1950, at Steepletop, her estate in Austerlitz, New York. When you visit today, you can wander a path through the woods and read her poems posted to trees along the way.

And as I looked a quickening gust
Of wind blew up to me and thrust
Into my face a miracle
Of orchard-breath, and with the smell, —
I know not how such things can be! —
I breathed my soul back into me.

— Edna St. Vincent Millay

recognize abundance
Abundance can be:
A bucket full of huckleberries.
A rolling carpet of acorns.
An expanse of electric blue sky.
Wonder.
Love.
What abundant gifts are you grateful for?

I am a guy who wanders around looking for nothing in particular, which is to say everything. In this frame of mind I have seen many things, in venues urban, suburban and rural. While ambling in the woods I have seen marten kits and three-legged elk and secret beds of watercress and the subtle dens of foxes. I have found thickets of wild grapevines, and hidden jungles of salmon-berries, and stands of huckleberries so remote and so delicious that it is a moral dilemma for me as to whether or not I should leave a map behind for my children when the time comes for me to add to the compost of the world.

— *Brian Doyle*

Nut trees, including oaks and beeches, are masters of abundance, producing massive amounts of nuts once every few years. These years of abundance are called "mast years." All the oaks or beeches or hickories in a region will choose the same year to rain down their riches. How do they know it is time? How does the message spread from one piece of fragmented forest to another? We don't yet know — it's a mystery.

One impulse from a vernal wood
May teach you more of man,
Of moral evil and of good,
Than all the sages can.

— William Wordsworth

stay humble

If we surrendered
to earth's intelligence
we could rise up rooted, like trees.

—Rainer Maria Rilke

The wisdom of nature is both wondrous
(when we comprehend it)
and mysterious (when we do not).

What do the trees know that we do not?

What ways of knowing are available to them
simply by way of being trees?

What can they teach us?

Consider that scientists don't fully understand
how trees do something as simple as draw water
all the way up from their roots to their leaves.
We can be grateful for the mysteries we have yet
to plumb and those we have yet to even think of.

Nature's creativity is infinite.

The H. J. Andrews Experimental Forest is a 16,000-acre site in the western Cascade mountains of Oregon and is home to ancient, old-growth cedar, hemlock, and Douglas fir. It is the site of long-term ecological research — but not just in science. Writing residencies bring poets and essayists to the forest to add their reflections and observations to the work being done here.

We need places that instill awe, fear, and trepidation — the old idea of the sublime. I came to the Andrews Forest in part to experience this mystery, to reconnect with some deeper part of my psyche that needs the occasional jolt from nature's less friendly side. To sense once again that we are part of something unknowable, and hence ungovernable.

— Frederick H. Swanson

Is it possible to be grateful even for what frightens and subdues us?

The Romantics of eighteenth- and nineteenth-century Europe often praised the "sublime" in nature: what is awe-inspiring and grand might be beautiful, yes, but it may also come with a tinge of terror.

The tree which moves some to tears of joy is in the eyes of others only a green thing that stands in the way. Some see nature all ridicule and deformity . . . and some scarce see nature at all. But to the eyes of the man of imagination, nature is imagination itself.

— William Blake

be
awed

An old-growth forest might embody the sublime, making us feel the largeness of time and space and the smallness and frailness of our human selves in comparison.

What place or experience makes you feel both awed and a little fearful at once?

Trees do not purr, do not flatter, do not inspire a craving for ownership or power. They stand their ground, immune to merely human urges.

— *Scott Russell Sanders*

---

offer thanks

Indeed, we have much to give thanks for:

from the tough, tiny intricacy of seeds to the heart-stopping grandeur of a towering redwood; from the beauty, inspiration, and vision that the trees lend us to all the ways they literally give us breath and life.

The Haudenosaunee people (also known as the Iroquois Confederacy, which includes the Mohawk, Oneida, Cayuga, Onondaga, Seneca, and Tuscarora) have a central prayer in their tradition called the Thanksgiving Address. They open and close all meetings with the address, thanking the many forces that sustain life and becoming spiritually tied to each.

As you walk in the woods or relax beneath a tree,

say a few silent thank-yous. Say them even in the face of sadness. Even in the face of grief.

We now turn our thoughts to the Trees. The Earth has many families of Trees who have their own instructions and uses. Some provide us with shelter and shade, others with fruit, beauty and other useful things. Many people of the world use a Tree as a symbol of peace and strength. With one mind, we send our greetings and our thanks to the Tree life.

Now our minds are one.

— *Haudenosaunee Thanksgiving Address*

Robin Wall Kimmerer, a biologist, writer,
and member of the Citizen Potawatomi Nation,
notes this remarkable thing about the generosity
of the natural world:

"Even a wounded world is feeding us.
Even a wounded world holds us,
giving us moments of wonder and joy."

Let us choose joy, but let's not stop there.

Let your joy and wonder also move you to reverence.
As you walk in the woods, think of the ground
you walk on as sacred. Make a little mental nod to all
the life you encounter, acknowledging each thing
as its own small miracle.

Every being has rights to be recognized and revered. Trees have tree rights, insects have insect rights, rivers have river rights, mountains have mountain rights.

— *Thomas Berry*

Although the trees may offer healing, we will not be fully healed until we, in turn, begin to heal the wounds we have inflicted on our landscapes.

We can honor the trees

and the earth with our wonder and our reverence, knowing that this is the foundation of a new relationship of reciprocity.

Writer Wendell Berry, who has long lived on a farm in Kentucky near where he grew up, lends his powerful voice to envisioning a stronger and healthier connection to place, community, and agriculture, and celebrating the interconnectedness of all things. Here is an excerpt from his playful but powerful "Manifesto: The Mad Farmer Liberation Front."

Invest in the millennium.

Plant sequoias.

Say that your main crop is the forest that you did not plant,

that you will not live to harvest.

Say that the leaves are harvested when they have rotted into the mold.

Call that profit. Prophesy such returns.

Put your faith in the two inches of humus that will build under the trees

every thousand years.

— Wendell Berry

yūgen
(Japanese)
a profound awareness,
beyond words, of the universe's
beauty and mystery

We are dreaming of a time when the land might give thanks for the people.

— Robin Wall Kimmerer

A posture of gratitude
is only the beginning.

ACKNOWLEDGMENTS

Many thanks to all my friends at Storey for making this book come to life, especially Deborah Balmuth, Liz Bevilacqua, Melinda Slaving, and creative kindred spirit Carolyn Eckert.

Also, I am aware that not everyone is comfortable and happy in the forest, and I am deeply grateful that I grew up with the privilege and opportunity to play and wander freely and safely in the woods. My wonderful parents wouldn't have had it any other way, and their love for the outdoors was contagious. Thanks to my two little sisters as well, who lovingly mocked me for my lonely teenage walks in the woods, and whose support means so much to me.

One sister once opined that I needed to find an "articulate outdoorsman" to marry (and accompany me on those walks) — so I did. Big thanks to my husband, Adam, for his insight and encouragement.

And finally, a giant hug to my son, Amos, whose fresh, wonder-filled view of the world helps me see it in new ways.

SOURCE CREDITS

34: Wright, Richard, Haiku #809, *Haiku: This Other World.* © 1998 by Wright. Reprinted by permission of Arcade Publishing, an imprint of Skyhorse Publishing, Inc. and John Hawkins and Associates, Inc.

36: Merwin, W. S., from "Place," *The Rain in the Trees.* © 1988 by W. S. Merwin. Used by permission of The Wylie Agency LLC and Alfred A. Knopf, an imprint of Knopf Doubleday Publishing Group, a division of Penguin Random House LLC. All rights reserved. Any third party use of this material, outside of this publication, is prohibited. Interested parties must apply directly to Penguin Random House LLC for permission.

37: Merwin, W. S., "High Fronds," *The Moon Before Morning.* © 2014 by W. S. Merwin. Reprinted with the permission of The Wylie Agency LLC and The Permission Company, Inc., on behalf of Copper Canyon Press, www.coppercanyonpress.org.

41: Gallagher, Tess, from "Walking Meditation with Thich Nhat Hanh," *Dear Ghosts.* © 2006 by Tess Gallagher. Reprinted with the permission of The Permissions Company, Inc., on behalf of Graywolf Press, Minneapolis, Minnesota, www.graywolfpress.org.

50: Caplan, Oliver, from *Krummholz Variations.* © 2016 Oliver Caplan Music, www.olivercaplan.com.

66, 83: Fries, Hannah, from "Descending Killington Peak" and "Naming the Trees," *Little Terrarium.* © 2016 by Hannah Fries.

81: Rogers, Pattiann, "Holy Heathen Rhapsody," *Holy Heathen Rhapsody.* © 2013 by Pattiann Rogers. Used by permission of Penguin Books, an imprint of Penguin Publishing Group, a division of Penguin Random House LLC. All rights reserved. Any third party use of this material, outside of this publication, is prohibited. Interested parties must apply directly to Penguin Random House LLC for permission.

85: Snyder, Gary, "Little Songs for Gaia," *Axe Handles.* © 1983 by Gary Snyder. Reprinted by permission of Counterpoint Press.

91: Merton, Thomas, from *Raids on the Unspeakable.* © 1966 by The Abbey of Gethsemani, Inc. Reprinted by permission of New Directions Publishing Corp.

102: Hirshfield, Jane, "Tree," *Given Sugar, Given Salt.* © 2001 by Jane Hirshfield. Reprinted by permission of HarperCollins Publishers.

117: Po, Li, "On the Mountain: A Conversation," *Bright Moon, Perching Birds: Poems.* Translation © 1987 by James Cryer and J. P. Seaton. Published by Wesleyan University Press. Used by permission.

129: Wood, Nancy, "My Help Is in the Mountain," *Hollering Sun.* © 1972 Nancy C. Wood. Courtesy of the Nancy Wood Literary Trust, www.NancyWood.com.

130: Issa, Kobayashi, "On a branch." Translation © Jane Hirshfield. Used with permission of Jane Hirshfield, all rights reserved.

138: Paley, Grace, "A Walk in March" first appeared in *The New Yorker.*

SOURCE CREDITS *continued*

150: cummings, e. e. "i thank You God for most this amazing." © 1950, 1978, 1991 by the Trustees for the E. E. Cummings Trust. © 1979 by George James Firmage, from *Complete Poems: 1904–1962* by E. E. Cummings, edited by George J. Firmage. Used by permission of Liveright Publishing Corporation.

152: Issa, Kobayashi, "What a strange thing!," *The Essential Haiku: Versions of Basho, Buson & Issa.* Edited and with an introduction by Robert Hass. Introduction and selection © 1994 by Robert Haas. Reprinted by permission of HarperCollins Publishers and Bloodaxe Books, www.bloodaxebooks.com.

166: Rilke, Rainer Maria, from "Wenn etwas mir vom Fenster fallt . . . / How surely gravity's law," *Rilke's Book of Hours*. Translation by Anita Barrows and Joanna Macy. © 1996 by Anita Barrows and Joanna Macy. Used by permission of Riverhead, an imprint of Penguin Publishing Group, a division of Penguin Random House LLC, and the translators. All rights reserved. Any third party use of this material, outside of this publication, is prohibited. Interested parties must apply directly to Penguin Random House LLC for permission.

183: Berry, Wendell, from "Manifesto: The Mad Farmer Liberation Front," *The Mad Farmer Poems.* © 2008 by Wendell Berry. Reprinted by permission of Counterpoint Press.

ADDITIONAL PHOTOGRAPHY CREDITS

Interior photography by Aaron Burden/Unsplash, 7 r., 30 t.r., 166; © Adam Brown, 50, 188; A. J. Gallagher/Unsplash, 23 t.l.; Alex Baber/Unsplash, 78 t.l.; © Alexey Kuzma/Stocksy United, 55 l.; Alexey Kuzmin/Unsplash, 68 b.l.; Ambambiinii/Unsplash, 58–59; Anders Jilden/Unsplash,178; Andreas Kind/Unsplash, 162; Andrew Coelho/Unsplash, 46–47; Anton Darius Sollers/Unsplash, 130–131; Autumn Mott/Unsplash, 45; Axel Van Der Donk/Unsplash, 134; Aya Okawa/Unsplash, 65 t.r.; Bartosz Bak/Unsplash, 135 b.r.; Becca Lavin/Unsplash, 154–155; Bintang Dwi Cahyo/Unspalsh, 180–181; © borchee/iStockphoto.com, 74–75; © Carol Adam/Getty Images, 44; Carolyn Eckert, 8, 11, 14, 23 t.r., 37, 55 r., 65 b.r., 71, 119, 147 b.l.; Casey Horner/Unsplash, 182; © Christian Schulze/EyeEm/Getty Images, 114–115; © Christina Rahr Lane, 13; Christopher Jolly/Unsplash, 176; © Cindy Loughridge, 88; Connor Limbocker/Unsplash, 23 b.l.; © Cosma Andrei/Stocksy United, 68 t.r., 174–175; © Cultura RM/Alamy Stock Photo, 60; © dagut/iStockphoto.com, 135 b.l.; © Damon D. Edwards 2018, 2; © Daring Wanderer/Stocksy United, 100; © Darren Muir/Stocksy United, 120–121; © Deirdre Malfatto/Stocksy United, 82; Denys Argyriou/Unsplash, 26–27; © Dietmar Humeny/EyeEm/Getty Images, 167; D. Jameson Rage/Unsplash, 30 b.l.; © Don Johnston_PP/Alamy Stock Photo, 67;

courtesy of The Edna St. Vincent Millay Society, 160; © Elyse Patten/Getty Images, 62 t.l.; © Emmanuel Davilma/EyeEm/Getty Images, 48; Emmanuel Hahn/Unsplash, 6 l.; © Emmanuel LATTES/Alamy Stock Photo, 92; © Eric Mueller, 24, 64 t., 77, 78 b.l., 112, 135 t.r.; © Erik Linton, 141; © Ethan Meleg/Getty Images, 83; © Evannovostro/ Shutterstock, 28; © Fe Langdon, 40; Filip Zrnzevic/ Unsplash, 170; © F. Verhelst, Papafrezzo Photography/Getty Images, 116; Geran De Klerk/ Unsplash, 192; © gracieross/iStockphoto.com, 104 b.r.; © heibaihui/iStockphoto.com, 117; © Helen Sotiriadis/Stocksy United, 104 t.r.; © HOWL/Stocksy United, 123, 142; Hunter Bryant/Unsplash, 128; Ian Keefe/Unsplash, 5; © Ivano De Santis/Alamy Stock Photo, 62 b.l.; © Javier Pardina/Stocksy United, 38, 53, 136; © Jess Lewis/Stocksy United, 159; Jon Flobrant/ Unsplash, 135 t.l.; Jonah Pettrich/Unsplash, 147 t.l.; Josh Post/Unsplash, 90; © Jovana Rikalo/ Stocksy United, 137; © Kondreddi Raghuram/ EyeEm/Getty Images, 68 t.l.; © Lawren Lu/Stocksy United, 34; © Lea Csontos/Stocksy United, 184; © Leander Nardin/Stocksy United, 149; © lighty25/ iStockphoto.com, 164 b.; Marcelo Silva/Unsplash, 6 r.; © marinuse — Oregon/Alamy Stock Photo, 72; © Mark Schulze, 168; © Mark Windom/Stocksy United, 104 b.l.; © Matteo Colombo/Stocksy United, 172; © Mawardi Bahar/Alamy Stock Photo, 30 b.r.; Mika Matin/Unsplash, 42–43; Morgan McBride/Unsplash, 147 t.r.; © mtruchon/ iStockphoto.com, 81; © Nate & Amanda Howard/ Stocksy United, 94, 103; © 2016 Oliver Caplan Music, www.olivercaplan.com, 51 music; © ooyoo/ Getty Images, 89; Oscar Sutton/Unsplash, 65 b.l.; © oxygen/Getty Images, 84; © Pansfun Images/ Stocksy United, 32; © Paul Edmondson/Stocksy United, 65 t.l., 78 b.r.; © Pete Leonard/Getty Images, 54; Peter Secan/Unsplash, 96; © Pgiam/ Getty Images, 62 t.r.; Ravi Roshan/Unsplash, 7 l.; © Razvan Cornel Constantin/Alamy Stock Photo, 30 t.l.; Redd Angelo/Unsplash, 152; Remi Walle/Unsplash, 68 b.r.; Ricardo Gomez Angel/ Unsplash, 171; © Robbie George/Getty Images, 33; Rodion Kutsaev/Unsplash, 3, 111; Roman Trifonov/ Unsplash, 124–125; © Ruth Black/Stocksy United, 107; © Sara Tekula/The Merwin Conservancy, 36; © sbk_20d pictures/Getty Images, 106; © Scott Barrow, 146; Seth Doyle/Unsplash, 23 b.r.; Shreyas Malavalli/Unsplash, 64 b.; © Siambizkit/ Shutterstock, 86; © skhoward/Getty Images, 62 b.r.; Stefan Steinbauer/Unsplash, 98–99; © Stephen Matera, 1, 126, 133, 156–157, 186–187; © Sydney Alford/Alamy Stock Photo, 51 background; Tanja Heffner/Unsplash, 151; © tbradford/ iStockphoto.com, 164 t.; Teemu Paananen/ Unsplash, 78 t.r.; Teodor Drobota/Unsplash, 147 b.r.; © TheYok/iStockphoto.com, 104 t.l.; © Winky Lewis, 80, 95

wander